Quilting

Around the World

Quilting
Around the World

Isabel Stanley and Jenny Watson

HERMES
HOUSE

This edition first published in 1997 by Hermes House
27 West 20th Street, New York, New York 10011

HERMES HOUSE books are available for bulk purchase for sales promotion
and for premium use. For details, please write or call the manager of special sales,
HERMES HOUSE, 27 West 20th Street, New York, New York 10011; (800) 354 9657.

Hermes House is an imprint of
Anness Publishing Limited

ISBN 1 901289 63 X

Publisher: Joanna Lorenz
Project Editor: Judith Simons
Assistant Editor: Daniel King
Text Editor: Judy Walker
Photographer: Gloria Nicol
Step Photographer: Lucy Tizard
Designer: Louise Morley
Illustrator: Lucinda Ganderton

Printed and bound in Hong Kong

1 3 5 7 9 10 8 6 4 2

CONTENTS

INTRODUCTION
· · · · ·

Interest in ethnic style has risen dramatically in the last 30 years. Adventurous travellers, amazed at the beauty and skill of indigenous craft objects, have brought them back to decorate their own homes. As well as being attractive souvenirs, these artifacts are steeped in local folklore. Traditions of ethnic decoration have endured the passage of time, whereas Western designs are constantly changing with the whims of fashion. The source for ethnic designs and the purpose of needlework are rooted in ancient beliefs. The decoration of textiles is extremely significant to tribal people, employing motifs which represent mythology and superstition. Potent symbols adorn embroidered and appliquéd garments, protecting the wearer from evil and bringing good fortune. Unusual talismans such as mirrors, pompons, coins and pieces of metal are used to distract and repel bad spirits.

Interest in ethnic textiles is not a new phenomenon and many traditions that have developed in the West were initiated by ideas brought over for trade and then adapted to suit Western tastes and needs. Such an example is corded quilting, which appears to have originated in the Middle East and travelled along the trade routes with merchants.

Ethnic craftspeople have in turn been influenced by Western innovations. This cross-exchange is manifested in both Hawaiian appliqué and Seminole patchwork. The Hawaiian appliqué technique evolved from a meeting of native women and American missionaries in 1820. The traditional design resembles a paper snowflake, and the fabric is folded and cut in the same way and then applied to a ground fabric. Inspiration for the designs comes from indigenous flora and fauna, and they are often quilted with stitches that echo the shape of the motif. The Seminole Indians of Florida developed their unique style of patchwork after the introduction of the sewing machine.

Appliqué has been practised worldwide for many centuries. It initially developed from a need to repair worn fabrics but it has developed into an art form in its own right. The oldest appliqué examples found are made from wool or hide date from BC. This type of appliqué is thought to have originated in the Northern hemisphere, because of its insulating properties. However, it also had a decorative element – in ancient Egypt appliqué was used to decorate funeral tents.

Indian textiles are probably the best known and loved, not only because of the country's popularity as a travel destination and the mysticism of the East, but also because of the beauty and variety of the textiles themselves. The Bengali kantha quilts have become favourite tourist souvenirs; layers of white cotton saris are decorated with motifs outlined in back stitch and filled with running stitches in red or blue thread. Imagery is drawn from the natural spirit world, with mythological beasts, animals and gods all depicted. The quilts are used as winter covers but also as wraps for precious books and objects. Appliqué hangings used as backdrops to religious gatherings and festivals have significant ceremonial importance and are usually made from silk and cotton saris. These hangings also featured reverse appliqué, in which areas of the applied fabric are cut away to reveal the layer below. The fabric to be applied is carefully folded and tacked (basted), slits are then cut into the layers and the work is opened out to reveal slightly irregular patterns. The raw edges are tucked under and slip-stitched to the ground fabric.

LEFT: A marriage of East and West. The style and fabric are definitely oriental, while the technique, shadow appliqué, is a Western invention.

The needlework techniques of the Hmong people of Laos, Vietnam and Thailand include embroidery and appliqué designs. Because of the delicacy of the work, the snipping is done while the stitching is in progress to create mazes that are derived from the patterns and rhythms of nature. The needlework is used to decorate hats, collars and the edgings of indigo-dyed jackets and trousers as well as bedcovers and cloths.

The most famous exponents of reverse appliqué are the Kuna Indian tribe of the San Blas islands, belonging to Panama. They use the technique to embellish molas, which are short-sleeved blouses. The vivid designs are eye-catching and unusual, featuring animals from Indian mythology and, oddly, political figures and slogans. This work is multi-layered, with each layer cut away to reveal the one below. The reverse inlay technique is also used. A frame and inlay are cut to the same size in contrasting fabrics and the inlay is appliquéd to its frame. A mola is identifiable by the narrow channels, dots and sawtooth lines.

Inlay appliqué exists as a technique on its own, used when bulkiness and strength are not required, or when the design should appear on both sides, as for banners. As the raw edges butt up against each other, fabrics of the same thickness are needed. Inlay appliqué may be made in two ways – the hand-sewn method in which the inlaid shape first has to be cut to fit the frame perfectly, or the machine-sewn method in which two layers are assembled, the outline stitched and the top fabric cut away to reveal the shape.

This book contains a variety of projects, featuring designs and techniques from all over the world. Some of the projects illustrated are lessons in traditional techniques, others are modern interpretations of ethnic themes. You may follow the projects or use the techniques for inspiration to channel into creative projects of your own. Whatever you choose you will bring something of a foreign culture and country into your life, not only in the finished item but also in the creative process.

BASIC TECHNIQUES

• • • • • •

The many varied projects in this book feature a wealth of design ideas employing a wide range of techniques, both old and modern, and from all over the world. You will discover the secrets of San Blas appliqué, Seminole patchwork and sashiko quilting, along with Pa Ndau design, echo quilting and much more. However, there are many standard quilting, patchwork and appliqué techniques that need to be grasped before you begin a project – you will be coming across the same methods again and again.

PATCHWORK TECHNIQUES

Pieced patchwork is made from fabric scraps that are cut into regular shapes and then sewn together in geometric patterns to form a mosaic of cloth. The patches can be pieced or joined together by one of two basic methods: by machine or by hand. Machining is quickest, but hand sewing gives a traditional look to a finished piece with slightly irregular seams. For the beginner, working over backing papers is the best way to make precise angled shapes when piecing by hand. Whichever method is chosen, accurate templates, meticulous measuring and cutting, careful stitching and thorough pressing are all vital for a professional finish.

TEMPLATES

Accurate templates will allow you to make patches identical in size and shape that will fit perfectly together. There are several different types of template you can make or buy. You can cut them yourself from card (cardboard) or from firm, clear plastic (acetate). Alternatively, you can make window templates, which allow you to view the fabric. Always make a new template for each shape required in a project – old templates eventually become a little distorted around the edges. Templates can also be purchased ready-made in various shapes and sizes.

Patchwork templates should always include a seam allowance; in this book the seam allowance is usually 5 mm (¼ in). If you are using backing papers, you will need to cut two templates if using card or plastic – one with the seam allowance included for marking the fabric and one without the seam allowance for the backing paper. If using a window template, the outside edge of the frame is used to mark the fabric and the inside edge of the frame the backing paper.

MAKING CARD (CARDBOARD) TEMPLATES

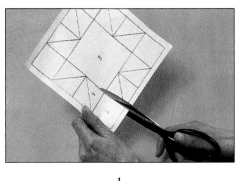

<u>1</u>

Transfer the design on to squared paper and cut around each shape with a sharp pair of scissors.

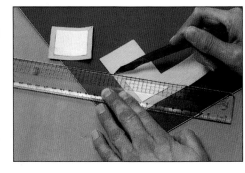

<u>2</u>

Glue the shapes to a piece of thin card (cardboard), and draw a seam allowance around each. Cut out the card.

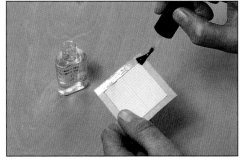

<u>3</u>

Protect the seam allowance area with a thin coat of clear nail varnish.

MAKING PLASTIC (ACETATE) TEMPLATES

Place the clear plastic (acetate) over the design and draw round each shape. Then draw a seam allowance round each and cut out. Being transparent, the template can be accurately positioned on the fabric.

MAKING WINDOW TEMPLATES

Trace the shape on to card (cardboard), then draw a 5 mm (¼ in) seam allowance round it. Cut out the outer and inner parts, leaving a card frame the exact width of the seam allowance.

MAKING CURVED TEMPLATES

For curved blocks, mark notches on the seam lines of the pattern before cutting it into sections. Cut out each template and then carefully cut out the notches with a craft knife.

PREPARING PATCHES

Position the template on the fabric, lining up one straight edge with the grain of the fabric. Draw round it on to the reverse of the fabric using a vanishing marker, tailor's chalk or a soft pencil. Butt the shapes together to ensure a good fit.

CUTTING OUT PATCHES IN GROUPS

1

Several patches can be cut at once using this method. Fold the fabric like a concertina and then staple the card (cardboard) template to the layers.

2

Use a sharp rotary cutter or a craft knife and press hard into the cutting mat.

3

Organize the cut pieces by stringing them on a length of thread. You can store them like this and remove them one at a time.

ATTACHING BACKING PAPERS

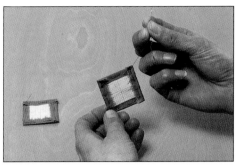

Pin the backing papers to the reverse of the fabric patches. Fold over or press the seam allowance. Leaving a short free end of thread, tack (baste) along the middle of the seam allowance to the end of the side and trim the corners. Fold over the adjacent seam allowance and continue to tack. Repeat on all sides, leaving the thread ends free so that the threads and the backing papers can be removed easily once the work has been pieced.

BACKING WITH INTERFACING

Iron-on interfacing can be used instead of backing papers. It is especially useful when machine piecing. Mark the patches on the interfacing adjacent to one another. Cut along the main lines first and then cut out the individual blocks. Iron these on to the reverse of the fabric, then mark a seam allowance round the interfacing on the fabric. Cut out the patches individually with scissors or as a group with a rotary cutter.

PIECING OR JOINING PATCHES

Lay out the cut patches to work out the final arrangement. When you are happy with the design, you can begin piecing the patches. There are several different methods of doing this, depending on whether you are piecing by hand or using a sewing machine.

HAND PIECING

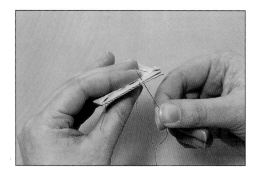

Right sides facing, pin the prepared patches together. First pin each corner, and then pin at equidistant points along the side. Join the patches with a small, neat whip stitch – or overstitch – as shown. Insert the needle in one corner and work across to the other, removing the pins as you go.

MACHINE PIECING PATCHES BY THE FLAG METHOD

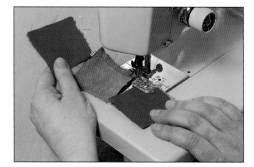

The flag method enables you to join several pairs of patches in one go. Right sides facing, pin the patches in pairs. Stitch along the seam line using the presser foot as a guide, removing the pins as you go. Leave a short uncut thread between each pair. Remove the flags and cut into units. Join enough pairs to make up the patched piece. To avoid bulk, always press the patch seams flat to one side and not open as in dressmaking.

JOINING PATCHES INTO ROWS

For both hand and machine piecing, make sure that the seam allowances match up perfectly before you pin and stitch the rows together. Press the seams in opposite directions to reduce bulk.

SETTING-IN — BOX PATCHWORK

Setting-in is the term used when a patch is sewn into an angle. To make the angled piece, stitch two pieces together along the seam line, stop stitching 5mm (¼ in) from the end of the seam, and secure with back stitch. Right sides facing, pin one angled piece to the edge of the patch. Stitch from the corner out to the edge, then swing the adjacent angled piece to the other side of the patch, again stitching from the corner out. Press the two seam allowances of the set-in patch toward the angled piece.

SASHING AND BORDERS

These are two very different things although they are cut and sewn in the same way. Sashings are fabric strips used within a design to separate individual patches, or blocks of patches. Borders go round the edges of the work to cover and hide any raw edges.

BLOCKED BORDERS

For the long sides of a border, cut the strips the same length as the quilt. For the short sides, cut the strips the width of the quilt plus the double width of the border. Right sides facing, sew the long strips to the piece first, and then the short strips. Press the seam allowance away from the direction of quilting.

BORDERS WITH MITRED CORNERS

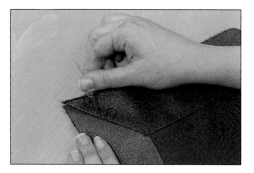

Cut the border strips as above, adding an extra 5 cm (2 in) to all four for mitring, and stitch to the quilt in the usual way. To mitre a corner by hand, press a border strip down at a 45 degree angle, pin and slip stitch on the right side to secure in place. To mitre by machine, work from the wrong side, pressing all the corners back at a 45 degree angle. Pin together and stitch along the fold. Trim the seam allowance and press flat.

LOG CABIN PATCHWORK

Always work from the middle out. Starting with a central square, pin and stitch strips to the square one by one, trimming each strip to the centre as you go. Work round the block anti-clockwise – each new strip will be slightly longer than the previous one. Continue adding strips until you reach the required size. Edge with mitred borders. Often several Log Cabin blocks are made and then stitched together to make a quilt.

QUILTING TECHNIQUES

Quilts are made from three layers: a top piece which is decorated, a layer of wadding (batting) for warmth and a backing piece. These layers are held together with lines of stitching which can be worked in a grid, straight rows or elaborate patterns. Quilted borders, medallions, knots and detailed corners are all possible. Originally, lines of tiny running stitches were worked to offer more warmth. Modern technology and new fibres have made this unnecessary, although the stitches still need to be of equal length.

TACKING (BASTING) QUILTS

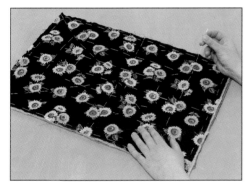

Sandwich the wadding (batting) between the top piece and the backing, with the fabrics right side out. Tack (baste) together securely. Knot a long length of thread in a contrasting colour. Work from the middle out, tacking the layers together horizontally, vertically and diagonally. If quilting by machine or with a hoop, add extra lines round the edges.

HAND QUILTING

Place the inner hoop on a flat surface, lay the tacked fabric on top. Place the outer hoop over both and screw the nut to tighten the hoop. Stitch from the top, using your free hand to guide the needle up and down through the layers below.

MACHINE QUILTING

For quilting grids and straight lines, a quilting foot will allow the machine to move more easily over thick fabrics. For free-form quilting, remove the foot and lower the foot lever. Stretch the fabric taut either with a hoop or your hands, and stitch slowly so that you can accurately guide the stitches.

Appliqué Techniques

Appliqué can be worked in a variety of fabrics, including silk, wool and cotton, and strong, closely woven fabric is possibly the best choice. Felt is popular for appliqué designs because it does not fray. Design ideas are limitless and virtually any shape can be used. San Blas appliqué and Hawaiian appliqué, together with cut and sew, inlaid and reverse appliqué methods, are just a few of the techniques featured in this book.

1

A quick and easy way to attach appliqué to the fabric. Because the appliqué fabric is fused to the web, it won't fray. Trace the outline on to the fusible web.

2

Roughly cut out the design and iron this on to the fabric. Cut round the outline with a sharp pair of scissors, a rotary cutter or craft knife.

3

Peel off the backing paper and iron, fusing the motif to the main fabric. Set the machine to a zig zag and stitch around the raw edge of the motif.

PIN TACKING (BASTING)

BELOW: This simple appliqué sunflower has been stitched on by hand.

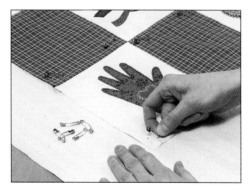

Tack (baste) the seam allowance around the appliqué design. Mark the placement lines on the right side of the fabric. Arrange the appliqué shapes on the fabric following these lines. First position the background pieces, and then layer any extra pieces on top. Alternatively, attach the pieces with double-sided tape.

STITCHES
· · · · · ·

Straight stitch is the standard machine sewing stitch, worked in straight lines and secured by back stitch at the end of each seam. Machine tacking stitches are worked by setting the machine to the longest stitch. To attach appliqué and crazy patchwork, set the machine to a close zig zag stitch and work a row of satin stitches. The following hand stitches are used throughout the book.

RUNNING STITCH

This is the main stitch used for hand quilting. It is also used for sewing seams in patchwork and quilting. Stitches should be of an even length, no bigger than 3 mm (⅛ in), and can be run a few at a time. Running stitch is also used in sashiko and kantha work.

HOLBEIN STITCH

Work a row of running stitch in one direction and then fill in the spaces on the return journey.

SLIP-STITCH

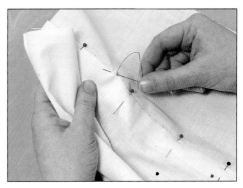

This stitch is used to secure a finished edge to another surface, like an appliqué or a binding. With the needle, catch a thread under the fabric together with a single thread on the fold of the fabric, spacing these small stitches evenly apart.

WHIP STITCH

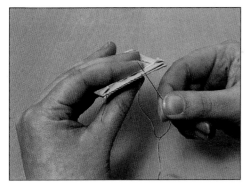

Also known as oversewing and overcasting, this small straight stitch is used to hold together two edges. Work from back to front, inserting the needle at an angle and picking up a thread from each piece at the same time.

STAB STITCH

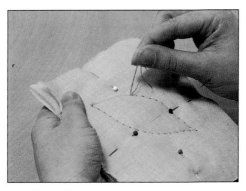

This stitch replaces running stitch when quilting thick fabric. Hold the needle perpendicular to the fabric, and work one stitch at a time. It is also used to outline individual shapes on quilted fabric.

BLANKET STITCH

Blanket, or buttonhole, stitch is ideal for finishing off raw or scalloped edges on fabrics that don't fray, such as felt or blanket. It can also be worked over a fold. Insert the needle into the back so that it points up to the raw edge, wind the loose thread over the needle and pull through the loop. Make a decorative feature of large blanket stitches by sewing them in a contrasting colour.

GENERAL TECHNIQUES

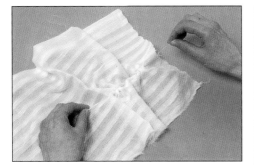

1

It is necessary to find the grain to straighten raw edges. Nick the fabric just below the raw edge, pull a thread gently across the fabric and cut along the line made. You can pull threads to fringe a piece of fabric and also to mark a grid. Sometimes you will need to find the straight grain in order to centre a motif.

Trace the motif on to squared paper. On another sheet of paper, mark out the same number of squares to the required size of the finished design. Copy the motif on to the new grid so that the lines of the design correspond exactly with the original.

Copy the design on to dressmaker's carbon paper. Place the carbon on the reverse of the fabric and then trace over the outline with a pen, pressing heavily.

2

Pouncing is used to transfer a design on to the right side of the fabric for an appliqué or quilting design. Trace over the design on to paper with a dressmaker's wheel or an unthreaded sewing machine, so that the design appears as a broken line. Push tailor's chalk through the pierced paper with a brush or sponge to mark the fabric.

BELOW: This drawstring bag shows designs transferred on to the patchwork squares.

3

Trace the design on to tissue paper, pin to the wrong side of the fabric then machine round the outline. Rip away the tissue paper to reveal the outline. This method is good for fine or fragile fabric.

MAKING AND USING BIAS STRIPS

Bias strips are used for binding, piping and also in the stained glass appliqué method. Cut a square on the straight grain, fold it in half diagonally and stitch together the open edges. Press the seam allowance flat and trim. Mark parallel lines on to the fabric and then roll it into a tube so that the top edge aligns with the first marked line. Pin and stitch along this line. Press the seam flat and trim. Cut along the marked lines into one long continuous strip of bias binding. Alternatively, cut several strips on the diagonal and then join them together, pressing the seam allowance flat.

BINDING A MITRED CORNER

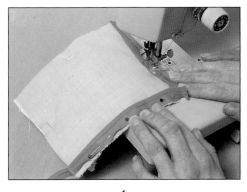

1

Stitch along one edge, reducing the size of the stitches near the corner. Stop stitching 5 mm (¼ in) from the corner, lift the presser foot and swivel the quilt to stitch the next edge. A tuck will form in the binding at the corner. Lower the presser foot, and carry on stitching the next side.

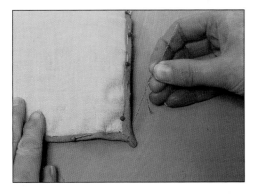

2

Fold over the binding, pin and sew close to the previous stitching line. Fold the tuck diagonally to mitre the corners and slip-stitch in place.

ENVELOPE CUSHION COVER

For the front, cut a square to fit the cushion pad, adding 1 cm (½ in) seam allowance on all sides. Cut a back piece 2.5 cm (1 in) bigger on one side, and then cut in half lengthways. Press, and sew a 1 cm (½ in) hem along the cut edge of both back pieces. Right sides facing, pin the front to the back pieces so that one hem lies slightly over the other. Sew round all four seams and, if directed, stitch in piping or fringing now. Clip the corners, press and turn right side out.

STRETCHING AND MOUNTING A PICTURE

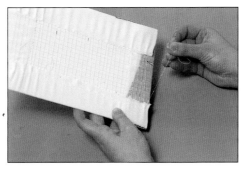

Stretch the finished piece taut over the backing. Using a strong thread, stitch back and forth, joining the raw edges in a criss cross pattern and pulling the thread tightly as you go. Work the long sides first, then repeat with the short sides. Secure to the backing board with tape.

DRAWSTRING BAG

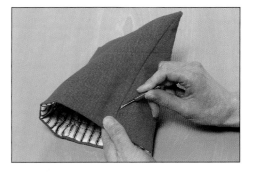

1

Pin together two rectangles in main fabric and sew round three sides, leaving the top short side open. Cut two rectangles the same size in lining and stitch the two long sides. Stitch part way across the short end, break off for 5 cm (2 in), then stitch to the end. Right sides facing, pin the two bags together and stitch a continuous line round the top edge. Trim and clip the seam. Pull the bag through the lining. Press and slip-stitch to close the gap.

2

Push the lining into the bag and press flat. For the channel, machine stitch two parallel lines, 1 cm (½ in) from the top edge and 1 cm (½ in) apart. Make a hole in the seam between the two rows of stitching with a stitch unpicker and thread the drawstring through.

PATCHWORK DUFFEL BAG

· · · · · ·

This colourful duffel bag is made from a piece of curved block patchwork. The curved blocks bend in opposite directions when placed together for sewing.

YOU WILL NEED
· · · · ·

50 cm (20 in) square turquoise cotton fabric

dressmaker's scissors

1 m x 90 cm (1 yd x 36 in) black cotton fabric

1 m x 90 cm (1 yd x 36 in) black lining fabric

paper and pencil

card (cardboard)

40 cm (16 in) square patterned cotton fabric

dressmaker's pins

sewing machine and matching thread

iron

80 cm (32 in) narrow piping cord

iron-on interfacing

60 cm (24 in) of 2 cm (¾ in) bias tape

needle and tacking (basting) thread

7 x 1 cm (½ in) brass rings

2 m (2 yd) thick cord

TO FINISH

Tack (baste) the lining to the patchwork, wrong sides facing. Join the base to the bag and, using the narrow piping cord and the black bias strips, bind with piping (see Basic Techniques). Iron interfacing to the turquoise top band, turn under a small hem at top and bottom and pin to the bag. Insert six evenly spaced, doubled-over pieces of tape and rings round the band, and top stitch in place. Sew the last ring to the base. Thread the thick cord through the six rings and then tie it to the bottom ring.

PREPARATION

The bag is made from 24 square blocks and measures 50 cm (20 in) deep by 75 cm (30 in). From the turquoise fabric, cut a top band 8 cm x 80 cm (3 in x 32 in). From the black cotton fabric, cut a circular base piece with a diameter of 30 cm (12 in), and bias strips for the piping. Cut the base to the same dimensions in the black lining fabric, then cut a lining measuring 55 cm x 85 cm (21½ in x 34 in).

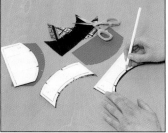

1

Trace the three templates from the back of the book on to card (cardboard). Cut out 24 pieces in each of the fabrics, using template 1 for the black, template 2 for the patterned fabric and template 3 for the turquoise fabric. Mark the notches and clip the curves (see Basic Techniques).

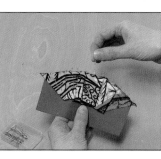

2

Working from the centre out, pin three different coloured pieces together between the notches to form a block. Repeat to make 24 blocks altogether. Stitch and press each block.

3

Lay out the blocks and arrange the design, alternating the curves as shown. Using the flag method (see Basic Techniques), sew into strips of four blocks. Sew the strips together to make one large patched piece, six blocks by four blocks.

CALICO BAG

· · · · · ·

The quilted base and pockets of this calico bag make it very strong, and so an ideal choice for travelling. When not in use, store bed linen in it for the spare room. The generous pockets can be filled with soap, towels and toothbrush to welcome your guest.

YOU WILL NEED

· · · · · ·

3 m x 90 cm (3 yd x 36 in) calico

50 cm x 90 cm (20 in x 36 in) cotton corduroy

1 m (1 yd) wadding (batting)

dressmaker's scissors

vanishing marker

dressmaker's pins

needle and tacking (basting) thread

sewing machine and matching thread

7 x 1 cm (½ in) eyelets (grommets)

2 m (2 yd) cotton rope

1

Place the wadding (batting) base circle between the corduroy and calico circles and tack (baste). Machine zig zag from the centre in a spiral. Tack the pocket piece, then zig zag lines up and down it. Remove the tacking threads.

2

Pin and stitch the bias calico strip to the base. Stitch the short strip of calico to the longest strip, fold over the small strip by 5 cm (2 in), tack and zig zag to make a square. Attach an eyelet (grommet).

3

Pin the pocket piece and strips to the lower edge of the bag with the eyelet (grommet) positioned centrally, and hanging 4 cm (1½ in) below the lower edge. Top stitch the strips to the bag.

PREPARATION

For the base, cut a circle of calico, corduroy and wadding (batting) 43 cm (17 in) in diameter. For the pockets, measure the circumference of the circle and cut a piece of calico the length of the circumference by 45 cm (18 in). Fold this lengthwise round a strip of wadding (batting) and pin. For the bag, cut another piece of calico the length of the circumference by 60 cm (24 in). Cut five calico strips 8 cm x 55 cm (3 in x 21½ in), one 8 cm x 65 cm (3 in x 26 in) and one 5 cm x 8 cm (2 in x 3 in). Cut a wide bias strip to fit the circumference of the base.

TO FINISH

Turn the top of the bag to the outside, first 1 cm (½ in), then 5 cm (2 in), and then another 5 cm (2 in). Press down and top stitch. Join the base to the bag and complete the binding. Attach pairs of eyelets (grommets) to the strips at the top of the bag, and thread with the rope.

CRAZY PATCHWORK PRAM QUILT

Crazy patches are a fun way to use up tiny scraps of fabric. However, like most patchwork, the best results are those which use a limited number of complementary colours and prints.

YOU WILL NEED

1 m x 90 cm (1 yd x 36 in) plain cotton fabric

dressmaker's scissors

assorted cotton scraps

iron

50 cm x 90 cm (20 in x 36 in) iron-on fusible bonding web

sewing machine and matching thread

70 cm x 90 cm 28 in x 36 in) wadding (batting)

70 cm x 90 cm 28 in x 36 in) backing fabric

PREPARATION

For the sashing, cut seven plain strips 21 cm x 7 cm (8¼ in x 2¾ in), and ten 21 cm x 8.5 cm (8¼ in x 3¼ in). Make up the sashing (see Basic Techniques). From the cotton scraps, cut two patterned pieces 7 cm (2¾ in) square, four 8.5 cm (3¼ in) square, and six 7 cm x 8.5 cm (2¾ in x 3¼ in). Cut the rest of the plain cotton into six 21 cm (8¼ in) squares.

TO FINISH

Sandwich the wadding (batting) between the patched piece and the backing. Tack (baste) the layers together. Trim the wadding to the finished edge and trim the backing to 2 cm (¾ in) from the edge. Turn the backing over to the top, and mitre the corners (see Basic Techniques).

1

Iron the fusible bonding web on to the plain cotton squares and peel off the backing paper. Arrange the fabric scraps on the surface of the bonding web. Butt the edges of the scraps together and iron in place.

2

Set the machine to zig zag and stitch the scraps to the squares. Sew the squares together in horizontal rows using the flag method (see Basic Techniques). Stitch the rows together then sew to the sashing.

CRIB QUILT

This pretty little quilt is made from twelve squares in an assortment of colours. It is appliquéd with naive animal and flower motifs. Choose an ethnic-inspired print for the backing fabric and motifs.

YOU WILL NEED

40 cm x 90 cm (16 in x 36 in) cream cotton fabric

20 cm x 90 cm (8 in x 36 in) green cotton fabric

20 cm x 90 cm (8 in x 36 in) yellow cotton fabric

dressmaker's scissors

card (cardboard) and pencil

craft knife

vanishing marker

scraps of iron-on fusible bonding web

iron

1 m x 90 cm (1 yd x 36 in) printed cotton fabric

sewing machine and matching thread

embroidery thread

crewel needle

1 m x 90 cm (1 yd x 36 in) calico

1 m (1 yd) wadding (batting)

PREPARATION

Cut the plain fabrics into 20 cm (8 in) squares: six cream, four green and two yellow. Enlarge the motifs and cut out in card (cardboard). Trace round the templates on to the bonding web and cut out. Iron to assorted scraps of the printed fabric and then cut out.

1

Iron the motifs to the plain cotton squares and appliqué with a machine zig zag stitch. Embellish the motifs with colourful embroidery.

FLOWER PETAL AND CENTRE 50%

ELEPHANT 50%

BIRD 50%

TO FINISH

Sew the squares together using the flag method (see Basic Techniques). Stitch horizontally into strips, then stitch the strips together. Cut the calico and wadding (batting) to the same size as the patchwork and cut the printed backing fabric 8 cm (3 in) larger all round. Bring the backing over to the front, mitre the corners (see Basic Techniques) and slip-stitch.

SAN BLAS OVEN MITTS

· · · · · ·

Layers of brightly coloured cotton are used to make these attractive oven mitts. The bird shape is cut away layer by layer, and stitched by hand to reveal a different colour each time. The designs used by the San Blas Indians usually feature birds and animals.

3

Cut away the red fabric inside the outline, leaving a small turning. Snip into the curves. Using red thread, turn under a small hem and slip-stitch through all layers.

PREPARATION

Cut a pattern piece in dressmaker's paper 75 cm x 18 cm (30 in x 7 in), and round off the ends. Cut one in red cotton, one in blue cotton and one in white felt. Mark the pattern piece 20 cm (8 in) from one end and cut along the marked line for the mitt. Cut out two in red, yellow and green fabric, four in blue fabric and four in white felt.

1

Layer the pattern pieces in two stacks: blue, yellow, green, blue and red. Separate the bottom blue pieces. Pin the rest together. Enlarge and trace the bird motif from the back of the book twice, reversing it the second time.

2

Cut out one paper bird motif and place it on one mitt. Draw round it in pencil. Tack (baste) an inner line, 5 mm (¼ in) from the pencil line, to show where to cut.

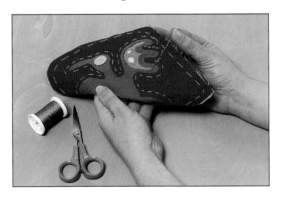

4

Draw the wings, head and tail on to the blue fabric. Cut away to reveal the green layer and hem in blue. Cut away to reveal the yellow wing details and hem in green thread. Remove the tacking stitches and press. Tack the reserved blue cotton piece to the last yellow piece as a lining. Bind the straight edge of the mitt with bias binding. Repeat for the second mitt, reversing the motif.

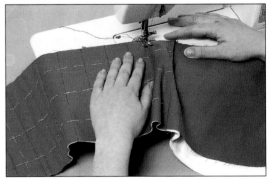

5

Tack pieces of cut felt to each end of the long felt strip. Lay this on the blue fabric with the extra felt next to the blue, and tack together. Mark a 4 cm (1½ in) grid along the length of the blue strip and machine quilt in red thread. Remove the tacking threads. Tack the red strip to the white felt. Lay the mitts with the blue lining facing the long red strip, tack and then sew close to the edge. Bind round the edges, then machine a bias binding loop to the join.

SAN BLAS CUSHION
......

This San Blas panel has been made up in brightly coloured cotton and sewn to a hessian (burlap) patch with a fringed border. The patch is then sewn on to a hessian cushion cover.

YOU WILL NEED
......

50 cm x 90 cm (20 in x 36 in) red cotton fabric

50 cm x 90 cm (20 in x 36 in) yellow cotton fabric

50 cm x 90 cm (20 in x 36 in) green cotton fabric

50 cm x 90 cm (20 in x 36 in) blue cotton fabric

dressmaker's scissors

paper and pencil

needle and tacking (basting) thread

crewel needle and yellow, blue, red, green and ecru embroidery thread

embroidery scissors

80 cm x 90 cm (32 in x 36 in) hessian (burlap)

dressmaker's pins

sewing machine and matching thread

40 cm (16 in) cushion pad

PREPARATION

Cut three red, two yellow, one green and one blue 20 cm (8 in) squares of fabric. Layer them red, yellow, green, red, yellow, blue, red, and tack (baste) together. Enlarge the motif and transfer to the fabric. Work the bird in San Blas appliqué (see San Blas Oven Mitts project). Machine a line 1 cm (½ in) from the edge of the patch and trim back. Cut out two pieces of hessian (burlap) 43 cm (17 in) square for the cover. Cut a hessian patch 28 cm (11 in) square.

1

Pin the bird motif on to the hessian (burlap) patch. Set the machine to zig zag and work satin stitch round the edge of the patch. With a pin draw the threads along all four sides to make the fringe. Make an envelope cushion cover to fit the pad (see Basic Techniques).

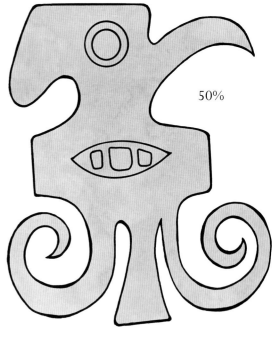

50%

SAN BLAS DRAWSTRING BAG

Nine patches are sewn together to make the front panel for this colourful drawstring bag. The animal motifs include a butterfly, a peacock and a fish, and are taken from traditional South American designs.

YOU WILL NEED

・・・・・・

45 cm x 71 cm (18 in x 28 in) red cotton fabric

sewing machine and red thread

25 cm x 90 cm (10 in x 36 in) red cotton fabric

25 cm x 90 cm (10 in x 36 in) yellow cotton fabric

25 cm x 90 cm (10 in x 36 in) blue cotton fabric

25 cm x 90 cm (10 in x 36 in) green cotton fabric

dressmaker's scissors

tracing paper and pencil

dressmaker's pins

crewel needle

red, yellow, blue and green embroidery thread

embroidery scissors

1 m (1 yd) thick cord

PREPARATION

To make the bag, fold over one of the long edges of the fabric by 5 cm (2 in), turn under a small hem and machine stitch. Cut the patchwork fabric into enough squares to make nine patches measuring 11 cm (4½ in) square. Layer the squares and tack (baste) together in stacks. Enlarge the motifs and transfer to the patches. Work the San Blas appliqué (see San Blas Oven Mitts project).

1

Join the patches in strips of three, then join the three strips to make a square.

TO FINISH

Pin the patchwork square to one side of the red fabric, parallel to the lower edge. Set the machine to zig zag and stitch the patchwork to the bag. Right sides facing, fold the bag in half and make up (see Basic Techniques). Thread the top channel with the cord and knot the ends.

50%

Child's San Blas Waistcoat

Here the reverse appliqué method is worked in a machine zig zag stitch to give a rich surface to two pockets, which are then used to decorate a child's waistcoat.

You Will Need

commercial waistcoat pattern to fit 61 cm (24 in) chest

50 cm x 90 cm (20 in x 36 in) red cotton fabric

50 cm x 90 cm (20 in x 36 in) yellow cotton fabric

dressmaker's scissors

25 cm (10 in) square green cotton fabric

25 cm (10 in) square blue cotton fabric

needle and tacking (basting) thread

paper and pencil

sewing machine and blue, yellow, green and red thread

embroidery scissors

crewel needle and red embroidery thread

dressmaker's pencil

Preparation

Cut out the waistcoat back and two fronts in both red and yellow fabric. For two pockets, cut out four red, three yellow, two green and two blue squares, each 12.5 cm (5 in) square. Trace the templates from the back of the book. For the frog, layer these blue, yellow, green, yellow, red. Tack (baste) together. For the snake, layer blue, yellow, red, green. Tack together. Enlarge the motifs on to paper and trace on to each pocket, adding a 1 cm (½ in) border.

1

To make the first pocket, machine stitch a line round the frog outline in blue. Cut away inside the stitching to reveal the yellow layer.

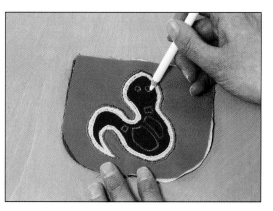

3

Draw the outline of a circle in the frog's middle and then draw on the eyes and a mouth. Stitch and cut away these to reveal yellow. Zig zag in green. Stitch a smaller circle in the middle and cut away to show the red. Zig zag in yellow.

To Finish

Press the pocket, turn right side out and slip-stitch the gap. Make the snake pocket to match. Pin and tack (baste) the pockets to the waistcoat fronts and attach with red half-cross stitches. Make up the waistcoat following the pattern instructions.

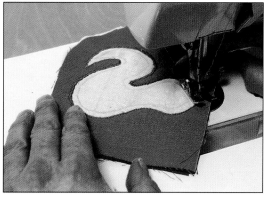

2

Zig zag stitch the raw edges in blue. Stitch inside the new outline in yellow and cut away as before to show green, then zig zag in yellow.

4

Right sides facing, stitch the red lining piece to the pocket, leaving a 5 cm (2 in) gap, and clip the curves.

Pocket Template 50%

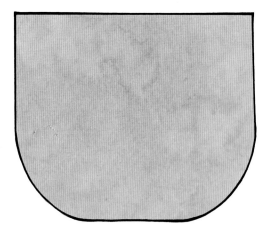

GREETINGS CARD
· · · · · ·

This patchwork technique is still used by the Seminole Indians to sew together strips of fabric, which are then cut into segments and re-sewn. Here paper strips are sewn together with a zig zag stitch to make a stunning design to appliqué on to a greetings card.

YOU WILL NEED
· · · · · ·

selection of coloured papers

pencil

paper scissors

sewing machine and matching thread

paper and pencil

card (cardboard)

paper varnish

75%

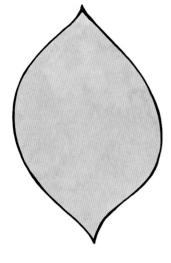

TO FINISH

Cut a piece of card (cardboard) 15 cm x 25 cm (6 in x 10 in) and fold in half widthways. Stitch the motif in place and varnish.

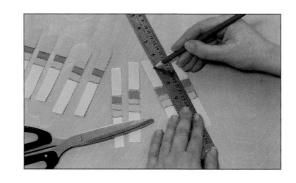

1

Measure and cut two strips of paper 3 cm (1¼ in) wide, and three strips 1 cm (½ in) wide. Arrange the three narrow strips between the two wide ones. Set the sewing machine to a medium zig zag. Overlap the strips and stitch together.

2

Cut into sections 1 cm (½ in) wide then offset the sections, matching the stitch lines so that they are staggered. Overlap and stitch together. Make two more shapes in the same way.

3

Cut two strips 3 cm (1¼ in) wide, two 1 cm (½ in) wide and a centre strip 2 cm (¾ in) wide. Arrange the narrow strips either side of the centre strip, and the wider strips outside these. Stitch and cut into 2 cm (¾ in) sections.

4

Cut 1 cm (½ in) strips. Offset and stagger the sections as before, matching the stitch lines. Insert the 1 cm (½ in) strips between the stitched sections, overlap and stitch.

5

Cut a strip across the highest and lowest points of the diamond. Arrange the narrow strip between two wide ones, overlap and stitch.

6

Enlarge the template and transfer to the patchwork piece, then cut out the motif.

NOTEBOOK COVER

This notebook has been covered with a piece of Seminole patchwork. The paper is cut on the diagonal, sewn and patched to form diamonds. Cover an address book and diary to make a matching set.

YOU WILL NEED
......

notebook

card (cardboard)

selection of coloured papers

pencil

craft knife

paper scissors

*sewing machine and
matching thread*

paper glue

paper varnish

PREPARATION

Open the notebook, lay it flat on a piece of card (cardboard) and draw round it. Using a ruler and craft knife, cut out the shape. Fold the card in half and press firmly along the fold line.

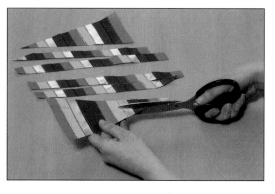

1

Measure the paper into strips 2 cm (¾ in) wide and cut out. Set the sewing machine to zig zag. Overlap the strips and stitch into one piece. Cut the piece into angled sections 2 cm (¾ in) wide, as shown.

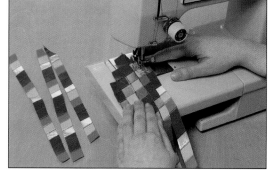

2

Overlap the sections so that they are staggered to form vertical diamond shapes. Use up all the sections. Stitch together.

TO FINISH

Cut the patchwork into a rectangle and glue it to the piece of card (cardboard). Leave to dry and then trim to size. Varnish the cover and when dry, glue to the notebook.

PADDED COAT HANGER

Padded coat hangers are a practical way to keep clothes in good shape. Make this piece of Seminole patchwork from satin ribbons – the end result will be very colourful.

YOU WILL NEED
......

37 cm (15 in) wooden coat hanger

tape measure

scrap of wadding (batting)

dressmaker's scissors

needle and tacking (basting) thread

5 cm x 50 cm (2 in x 20 in) satin ribbon in three colours

sewing machine and matching thread

vanishing marker

scraps of ribbon

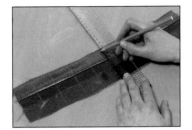

1
Machine the ribbons together. Mark across every 5 cm (2 in) and cut into strips.

2
Arrange the strips, offsetting them so that they are staggered. Reverse every other strip. Make two patches of equal length. Right sides facing, stitch them together round the edges, leaving a gap on the top edge.

3
Turn right side out and cover the hanger. Turn under a hem on the raw edges and slip-stitch.

PREPARATION

Measure the coat hanger and cut a piece of wadding (batting) to fit. Wrap round the hanger and tack (baste) the long edges together.

TO FINISH

Wrap the metal hook with a length of ribbon and slip-stitch in place. Decorate with contrasting ribbon.

GIFT TAGS
· · · · · ·

These gift tags are made from patchwork strips cut from plain coloured paper. Patterned gift wrapping paper could also be used in the same way to make an interesting piece of Seminole patchwork.

YOU WILL NEED
· · · · · ·

selection of coloured papers

paper scissors

sewing machine and matching thread

card (cardboard)

paper glue

paper varnish

hole punch

scraps of ribbon

DESIGN A PREPARATION

Cut two strips of paper in one colour 2 cm (¾ in) wide and one contrasting strip 1 cm (½ in) wide. Arrange the narrow strip between the wide ones. Overlap and machine zig zag stitch together. Next cut two strips 2 cm (¾ in) wide in two different colours, and one strip in a third colour 1 cm (½ in) wide. Arrange and stitch as before.

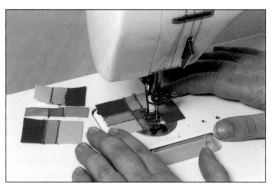

1
Cut the first patch into strips 1 cm (½ in) wide, and the second into strips 2 cm (¾ in) wide.

2
Arrange as shown, with one narrow strip placed between two wide ones, then stitch.

DESIGN B PREPARATION

Cut two strips of paper in two different colours 2 cm (¾ in) wide, and two strips in two more colours 1 cm (½ in) wide. Arrange the narrow strips between the wide ones. Overlap and machine zig zag stitch together. Next cut three strips of paper in different colours, one 3 cm (1¼ in), one 2 cm (¾ in) and one 1 cm (½ in) wide. Stitch the narrow strip between the two wide ones.

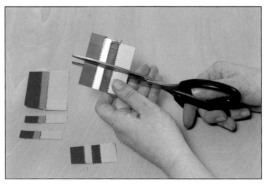

1
Cut one patch into strips 2 cm (¾ in) wide, and one into strips 1 cm (½ in) wide.

2
Arrange as shown, with two narrow strips placed between two wide ones, then stitch.

TO FINISH

Cut two pieces of card (cardboard) to size and glue on to the paper patches. Varnish and leave to dry. Punch a hole in one corner of each card and thread with ribbon.

SASHIKO QUILT

Sashiko quilting originated in Japan in the 18th century as protective clothing worn by firemen. The wadding (batting) is held between two layers of indigo fabric with white running stitches – the closer the stitches, the more durable the garment.

YOU WILL NEED
• • • • • •

card (cardboard}

pencil

craft knife

*2 m x 90 cm (2¼ yd x 36 in)
assorted plain and print
cotton fabrics*

dressmaker's scissors

*1.3 m x 1.6 m (52 in x
64 in) wadding (batting)*

*sewing machine and
matching thread*

iron

dressmaker's pins

*1.3 m x 1.6 m (52 in x
64 in) cotton backing*

vanishing marker

white quilting thread

crewel needle

PREPARATION

Make three card (cardboard) templates, one 11 cm (4½ in) square, one 5 cm (2 in) square and one 3 cm (1¼ in) square. Using the 11 cm (4½ in) template, cut the plain and print fabrics into 180 squares.

1
Using the two smaller card templates, draw three squares on each plain fabric square – two diagonal to the fabric square, and repeat the smallest square as a square on top of the smallest diagonal.

2
Lay the squares 12 across and 15 down. Stitch in horizontal rows using the flag method (see Basic Techniques). Press the seams in opposite directions. Stitch the strips together.

3
Sandwich the wadding (batting) between the patched piece and the cotton backing. Pin and tack (baste) the layers together (see Basic Techniques). Quilt along the marked lines in white thread using running stitch.

TO FINISH

Trim the wadding (batting) back to the finished edge and trim the backing to 2 cm (¾ in) from the edge. Turn the backing over to the top, mitre the corners and slip-stitch.

SASHIKO BAG

· · · · · ·

A small piece of sashiko quilting is easy to transform into an envelope bag. First make the quilted square then follow the instructions to make the bag.

PREPARATION

Cut the blue fabric into two pieces 1 m (1 yd) square. Mark a 75 cm (30 in) square in the centre of one blue square. Mark a diamond pattern to fill the central square. Sandwich the wadding (batting) between the two cotton squares and tack (baste), first round the edges then working from the middle out.

1

Work a row of running stitches in quilting thread diagonally across the marked square. Work the diamond pattern, making the same number of stitches in each section. At the intersections, miss a stitch.

2

Work tiny running stitches in rows of parallel lines round the borders.

3

Machine stitch the binding to the wrong side round the edges. Pull the four corners together and stitch two seams with the binding sandwiched between, facing the right side. Fold over binding on the remaining sides and top stitch. Fasten the bag with a thread loop and a bead or button.

PATCHWORK CURTAIN

· · · · · ·

Checked and appliquéd patches are arranged diagonally in a checker board design for this curtain. Choose a bold, ethnic design to complete the look.

YOU WILL NEED
· · · · ·

tape measure

dyed calico, in two colours (see Preparation below)

dressmaker's scissors

50 cm x 90 cm (20 in x 36 in) iron-on interfacing

dressmaker's pins

sewing machine and matching thread

paper and pencil

scraps of cotton fabric, for the appliqué

needle and thread

curtain tape, to fit the curtain width plus 2.5 cm (1 in)

curtain hooks

1

Draw a bold, ethnic-inspired design on paper, or copy ours from the picture. Cut out each shape in fabric scraps and iron interfacing on to the back. Pin to the plain calico squares.

2

Tack (baste), then appliqué each shape with machine zig zag stitch on to the plain calico squares to secure in place.

PREPARATION

To calculate how much fabric you will need, measure the window and multiply by three. For the drop, add an extra 10 cm (4 in) to the length. Cut some calico in one colour into 30 cm (12 in) squares. Arrange them on the floor checker board style to the size of the curtain. Cut a few squares diagonally in half to make triangles for the edges. Cut the interfacing into 30 cm (12 in) squares. Then cut 10 cm (4 in) squares in both calico colours, and arrange and pin groups of nine squares to the interfacing. Zig zag stitch over the raw edges. Make enough checked squares to complete the curtain.

TO FINISH

Using the flag method (see Basic Techniques), join the squares in strips then join the strips. Turn a small machine hem on both long sides of the curtain. Press the top under 1 cm (½ in) and, with wrong sides facing, tack (baste) on the curtain tape. Stitch. Turn under a hem on the bottom edge and slip-stitch. Attach the curtain hooks. Repeat if you wish to make a pair of curtains.

BOLSTER CUSHION

This small bolster cushion is made from calico and ribbed silk. A pattern of slashes is cut into the top silk fabric and neatly hemmed to the calico under-cover. This creates the interesting texture, which is complemented by fringing.

YOU WILL NEED
• • • • • •

paper and pencil

70 cm x 90 cm (28 in x 36 in) calico

70 cm x 90 cm (28 in x 36 in) raw silk

dressmaker's scissors

vanishing marker

sharp scissors

iron

needle and tacking (basting) thread

sewing machine and matching thread

wadding (batting)

PREPARATION

Cut a paper template for the main piece. Cut out in both calico and silk. For the base, cut two in each fabric. To make the frayed fringe, cut two strips of calico, 5 cm x 55 cm (2 in x 21½ in).

TO FINISH

Right sides facing, stitch the short ends to make a tube, leaving a 10 cm (4 in) gap in the middle for turning. Tack (baste) the fringe strips each end of the tube. Stitch the base pieces to the tube. Turn the bolster right side out and fray the calico down to the seam line using a needle. Fill the bolster with wadding (batting) and slip-stitch the opening closed.

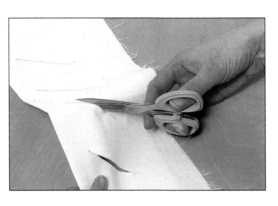

1

Transfer the slash line design to the calico with a vanishing marker and cut with sharp scissors.

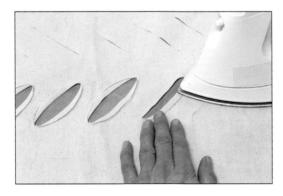

2

Turn under a small hem on each of the slash lines and press on to the wrong side. Tack (baste) the calico to the silk round the almond shapes.

3

Slip-stitch round the almond shapes. Press flat on the wrong side.

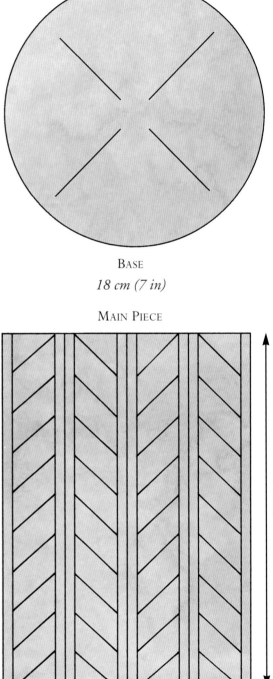

BASE
18 cm (7 in)

MAIN PIECE

50 cm (20 in)

40 cm (16 in)

APPLIQUÉ FELT BALL
· · · · · ·

This soft ball is safe to play with and big enough for a baby to hold easily. It is decorated with colourful appliqué shapes worked in simple embroidery stitches.

YOU WILL NEED
· · · · · ·

paper and pencil
card (cardboard)
craft knife
20 cm x 90 cm
(8 in x 36 in) calico
dressmaker's scissors
scraps of coloured felt
dressmaker's pins
embroidery hoop
assorted embroidery threads
crewel needle
needle and matching thread
wadding (batting)
scrap of ribbon, optional

PREPARATION

Trace the pentagon and make 12 templates in thin card (cardboard). Draw 12 pentagons on the calico, spacing them at least 2.5 cm (1 in) apart, but do not cut out. Make heart and petal templates and cut out in coloured felt. Cut two sizes of small circles for the flower centres.

1

Pin a circle and heart to one pentagon. Place the calico in the embroidery hoop. Work a running stitch round the heart. Stitch an asterisk to hold the circle in place. Appliqué all the pentagons in this way.

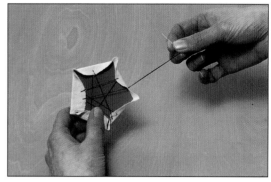

2

Cut out the pentagons, adding a 1 cm (½ in) seam allowance. Stretch the calico patches over the templates (see Basic Techniques).

3

Whip stitch five patches to one central patch to make half a ball. Repeat for the second half.

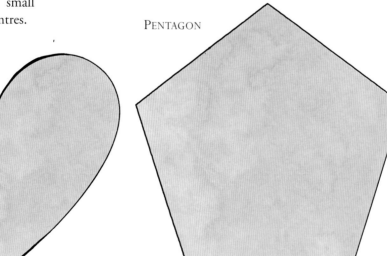

4

Stitch the two halves together, leaving three seams unsewn. Remove the templates.

TO FINISH

Fill with wadding (batting) and close the last seams. If you wish, insert a small ribbon loop into the last seam to hang the ball.

PENTAGON

HEART

PETAL

BABY BLANKET
. . . . . .

This is another example of inlaid appliqué. Here the method is used to stitch a bird motif on to a baby's blanket. The motif is then decorated with brightly coloured embroidery threads.

YOU WILL NEED
. . . . . .

wool blanket

dressmaker's scissors

paper and pencil

card (cardboard)

craft knife

scraps of coloured blanket fabric

dressmaker's pins

vanishing marker

needle and tacking (basting) thread

sharp scissors

sewing machine and contrasting thread

iron

assorted embroidery threads

crewel needle

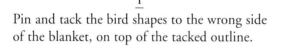

1
Pin and tack the bird shapes to the wrong side of the blanket, on top of the tacked outline.

2
From the right side, carefully cut the fabric along the outline.

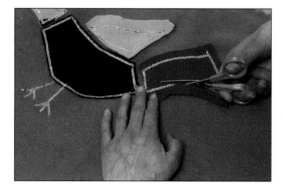

3
Set the machine to zig zag, pin a piece of paper to the wrong side of the appliqué pieces and work a wide satin stitch over the raw edges. Stitch the bird's legs, as shown. Trim away any excess fabric.

4
Press under a narrow hem all round the blanket and stitch with a wide blanket stitch in contrasting thread. Hand stitch details on to the bird using embroidery threads.

PREPARATION

Cut the blanket to the required size for a cot (crib) or child's bed. Enlarge and trace the bird motif and cut templates in card (cardboard). Cut out the shapes in coloured fabric, adding a 2 cm (¾ in) seam allowance. Position the templates on the right side of the blanket and draw round. Tack (baste) carefully over the line.

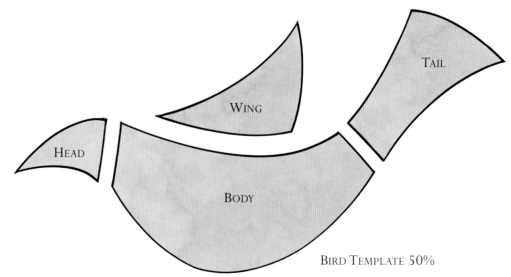

HEAD

WING

TAIL

BODY

BIRD TEMPLATE 50%

SEMINOLE TOWEL

A geometric patchwork piece, cut into narrow strips then stitched in rows, makes an attractive border for a bathroom towel.

YOU WILL NEED
• • • • • •

12 cm x 90 cm (5 in x 36 in) cotton fabric in two colours

vanishing marker

dressmaker's scissors

iron

scrap of iron-on fusible bonding web

sewing machine and matching thread

20 cm x 90 cm (8 in x 36 in) backing fabric

dressmaker's pins

bath towel

PREPARATION

Cut both cotton fabrics into three strips 6 cm x 40 cm (2½ in x 16 in), and iron to the bonding web. Alternate the colours so that the strips overlap. Machine together with a zig zag stitch to make one piece of patchwork.

1

Cut the patchwork into strips 2 cm (¾ in) wide. Offset the strips on a piece of backing fabric as shown and iron on. Secure with a zig zag stitch.

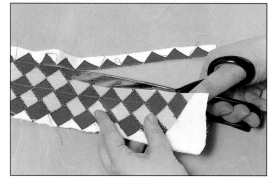

2

Mark a horizontal line through the centre of the diamonds and cut into long strips.

3

Pin several strips to each end of the towel, running parallel to the edge. Machine in place.

QUILTED EGG COSY

· · · · · ·

This egg cosy is a tiny copy of a traditional Nepalese hat. It is quilted in cotton fabric with white thread and topped with a woollen tassel.

YOU WILL NEED

· · · · · ·

card (cardboard) and pencil

craft knife

dressmaker's scissors

18 cm x 24 cm (7 in x 9½ in) plain cotton fabric

18 cm x 24 cm (7 in x 9½ in) lining fabric, in contrasting colour

15 cm x 20 cm (6 in x 8 in) wadding (batting)

needle and tacking (basting) thread

vanishing marker

white quilting thread

crewel needle

embroidery scissors

sewing machine and matching thread

scraps of knitting wool

PREPARATION

Enlarge the template and cut out in card (cardboard). Cut out two pieces in both cotton and lining, adding a 1 cm (½ in) seam allowance all round. Cut out two pieces in wadding (batting), without any seam allowance, and sandwich each between the cotton and the lining. Tack (baste) the layers together (see Basic Techniques). Mark a geometric design, in freehand, on to both cotton shapes.

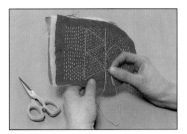

1

Work over the design in small, neat running stitches with quilting thread, filling the whole area. Make the second side the same.

2

Trim the top fabric back to the wadding. Bind the lower edge with lining fabric and top-stitch. Right sides facing, stitch round the seam line.

3

Cut a piece of card (cardboard) 1 cm x 2.5 cm (½ in x 1 in) and wind lengths of knitting wool round it several times. The more you wind, the thicker the tassel.

50%

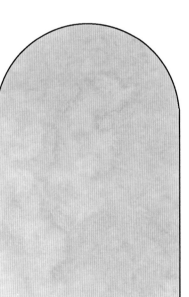

TO FINISH

Pull the wool carefully off the card (cardboard) and secure at the top with a short length of wool. Splice the wool through the other end of the loop, and trim. Bind the uncut strands together at the top. Stitch the tassel to the top of the finished egg cosy.

Pa Ndau Appliqué Frame

· · · · · ·

An elaborate maze design from the Hmong people of South East Asia, known as "crooked road" or "frog's legs". This normally complicated appliqué technique is simplified here.

YOU WILL NEED
· · · · · ·

dressmaker's scissors

45 cm x 90 cm (18 in x 36 in) black cotton fabric

30 cm x 60 cm (12 in x 24 in) white cotton fabric

45 cm (18 in) square graph paper

pencil

thick black pen

spray starch

iron

vanishing marker

dressmaker's pins

needle and matching thread

embroidery scissors

two mount board squares, 17.5 cm (6¾ in) square and 16.5 cm (6½ in) square

double-sided tape

fabric glue

brass curtain ring

PREPARATION

Cut the black fabric in half to make two pieces 45 cm (18 in) square, and the white fabric to make two pieces 30 cm (12 in) square.

1

Trace the template from the back of the book on to graph paper and fill in the lines of the design with thick black pen. Spray both sides of one white square with starch and press. Lay the fabric on top of the graph paper and mark the corners of the design with the vanishing marker.

2

Place one square of black cotton between the two white squares with the marked one uppermost. Pin and tack (baste) around the inside and outside edges of the fabric frame. Tack (baste) crossways in the middle of each side. Cutting one section at a time, make a slit in the outside black line, always keeping the line central. Snip into the corners.

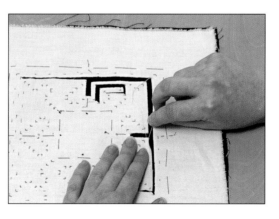

3

Using the point of the needle, fold under a tiny turning and slip-stitch a hem. Stitch closer together at the corners. Work the whole frame one quarter at a time. Use the corner marks as guidelines and keep referring back to the original design.

4

Pin a small hem on the outside and inside edges of the finished piece. Cut a 6 cm (2½ in) square in the centre of the large mount board. Lay the appliqué face down and cut into the corners of the window. Stretch the white fabric on to double-sided tape. Glue the black fabric to cover the small square. Place together and slip-stitch the sides. Sew a brass ring to the top.

Pa Ndau Appliqué Box Lid

Another simplified design from the Hmong tribes, created with a stencil. Enlarge the design if you want to cover a different-sized box.

You Will Need
. . . . . .

25 cm x 50 cm (10 in x 20 in) red cotton fabric

dressmaker's scissors

paper and pencil

paper scissors

wooden box, 14 cm (5½ in) square

spray starch

iron

25 cm (10 in) square yellow cotton fabric

vanishing marker

embroidery scissors

needle and matching thread

14 cm (5½ in) square wadding (batting)

fabric glue

double-sided tape

corded red ribbon

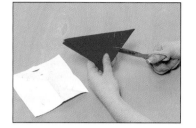

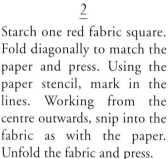

1
Cut the red fabric into two pieces 25 cm (10 in) square. Cut a square of paper to fit the lid. Halve diagonally, and then halve again. Trace the design. Snip into each line, open out to check the pattern and then refold the stencil.

2
Starch one red fabric square. Fold diagonally to match the paper and press. Using the paper stencil, mark in the lines. Working from the centre outwards, snip into the fabric as with the paper. Unfold the fabric and press.

3
Place the cut fabric on to the yellow and red squares. Tack (baste) 1 cm (½ in) away from the snipped fabric. Cut along the lines between snips, cutting two lines at a time. Turn a small hem on the outside edge. Snip into the V's at the inner edge, turn a hem and slip-stitch.

4
Draw four 5 mm (¼ in) quarter circles in the centre of the appliqué. Snip into the corners, turn under a small hem and slip-stitch. Remove any remaining tacking stitches and press.

5
Glue the wadding (batting) to the lid, and stick tape round the top of the box. Trim the appliqué to 16 cm (6¼ in), stretch over the lid and on to the tape. Mitre the corners and stick more tape to the sides. Glue red ribbon on top to finish.

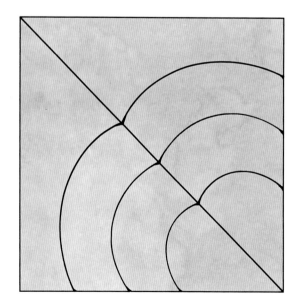

CALICO NAPKIN

This homemade napkin is appliquéd and stitched by hand. Alternatively, appliqué the simple motif on to ready-made napkins.

YOU WILL NEED

card (cardboard) and pencil

craft knife

fabric scraps in blue, pink, cream and green

dressmaker's scissors

48 cm (19 in) square calico

tailor's chalk

scrap of iron-on fusible bonding web

iron

dressmaker's pins

green and blue embroidery thread

crewel needle

PREPARATION

Enlarge the heart motif and make a card (cardboard) template. Cut out in blue fabric, adding a 1 cm (½ in) seam allowance. Press under a small hem on the heart and the calico square. Draw the flower and leaves freehand on to the bonding web and cut out. Iron the shapes on to the scraps. Cut out, pin and iron on to the heart.

1

Embroider a green stalk and randomly appliqué the shapes on to the heart. Pin and appliqué the heart to a corner of the napkin.

2

Fill the heart with running stitches then finish the edges of the napkin with a decorative running stitch border.

50%

TABLE MATS

· · · · · ·

These simple table mats look particularly effective if made in a rough-textured cotton fabric. They are
decorated with fringed edges and simple running stitches worked in colourful threads,
which hold the wadding (batting) in place.

YOU WILL NEED
· · · · · ·

*2 m x 90 cm (2¼ yd x 36 in)
checked cotton fabric*

dressmaker's scissors

1 m (1 yd) wadding (batting)

*needle and tacking
(basting) thread*

assorted embroidery threads

crewel needle

*sewing machine and
matching thread*

iron

PREPARATION

Cut the fabric into eight
pieces, each measuring 50 cm
x 45 cm (20 in x 18 in). Cut
the wadding (batting) into
four pieces 40 cm x 36 cm
(16 in x 14 in). Sandwich the
wadding between two pieces
of fabric, leaving a 5 cm (2 in)
overlap on all sides. Tack
(baste) one piece of fabric to
the wadding, then turn over
and repeat with the second
piece of fabric.

TO FINISH

Press the mats flat and trim
any stray threads.

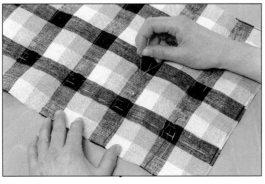

1

Work rows of running stitch in parallel lines
right across the mat. Sew through all the layers,
changing colours as you go. Remove the
tacking (basting) threads.

2

Machine stitch a line round the mat, 5 cm
(2 in) from the raw edges. With a needle, pull
threads to fringe the edges. Repeat for the other
three mats.

WOOL HAT

This hat with a turn-back border is made from blanket fabric, and ties in a knot at the crown. The inlaid appliqué motifs which run round the border are whip stitched in a contrasting colour.

YOU WILL NEED
• • • • • •

*40 cm x 90 cm
(16 in x 36 in) woollen
blanket fabric*

dressmaker's scissors

paper and pencil

card (cardboard)

craft knife

vanishing marker

*scraps of woollen blanket
fabric in two colours*

*60 cm x 5 cm (24 in x 2 in)
iron-on interfacing*

iron

needle and contrasting thread

*sewing machine and
matching thread*

PREPARATION

Cut a piece of fabric 60 cm x 40 cm (24 in x 16 in). Turn under a double hem, 2 cm (¾ in) wide, and machine stitch. Cut two ties 23 cm x 5 cm (9 in x 2 in). Trace and cut templates out of card (cardboard).

1

Alternate the two templates along the hem, drawing round them. Cut out the shapes.

2

Draw the shapes on to the wool scraps, and cut out an equal number in each colour. Lay a cut motif into a corresponding shape and iron the interfacing over it. Work along the hem fusing the interfacing to the fabric as you go.

3

Right sides facing, whip stitch over the cut edges in a contrasting colour (see Basic Techniques). Fold the hat in half and machine the top and back seams.

4

To make the ties, press under both long and one short edge, fold in half lengthways and zig zag round the edges. Slip the raw ends into each top corner of the hat. Turn back the appliquéd border and slip-stitch to the hat. Stitch the ties to the top seam and tie in a knot.

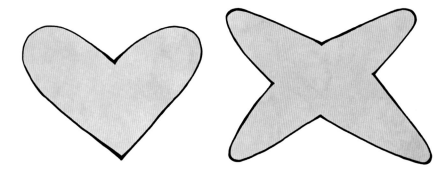

BABY'S APPLIQUÉD CARDIGAN
. . . . . .

Felt animal motifs reminiscent of mola work are appliquéd with tiny blanket stitches in a contrasting colour. Knit this patchwork cardigan, or buy one ready-made.

YOU WILL NEED
. . . . . .

3 x 25 g (1 oz) balls random-dyed red yarn

1 x 25 g (1 oz) ball in two contrasting shades

4 mm (No 8) knitting needles

white, red and navy felt

dressmaker's scissors

needle and tacking (basting) thread

paper and pencil

embroidery scissors

dressmaker's pins

white, red and navy embroidery thread

crewel needle

TO FIT: 50 cm (20 in) chest
ACTUAL SIZE: 58 cm (23 in)
LENGTH: 29 cm (11½ in)
SLEEVE LENGTH: 23 cm (9 in)

PREPARATION

Tension: worked in stocking stitch on 4 mm (No 8) needles, 20 sts x 24 rows measures 10 cm (4 in). Knit the cardigan as follows.
Back: knit a piece 52 sts wide by 32 cm (13 in) long, with a 1 cm (½ in) border and divided into 16 patches, each 13 sts wide by 7 cm (2¾ in) deep.
Fronts: cast on 26 sts and work in patches, as back. Knit straight to 15 cm (6 in). Shape the neck by decreasing 9 sts on one edge over the remaining rows. Reverse the shapings for the other front.
Sleeves: cast on 39 sts and work a 2 cm (¾ in) border. The sleeves are divided into nine patches. Press lightly. Sew the shoulder seams and set in the sleeves. Sew the side and sleeve seams.
Cut the felt into 10 cm (4 in) squares and layer red/white/red or navy/white/navy and tack (baste). Cut one stack for each front and each sleeve.

1
Trace the motifs from the back of the book on to paper and then transfer to felt. Cut out the felt shapes, cutting a wide base layer, and cut eyes and mouth from the top layer. Pin and tack (baste) the first shape to the cardigan. Working in layers, secure with small blanket stitches in contrasting coloured threads.

2
For the fastenings, cut four 2.5 cm (1 in) squares in white felt and fold in half to make triangles. Place the straight folded edge to the front edge of the cardigan and pin. Blanket stitch round two sides of the triangle in red.

3
For each tie, cut three 28 cm (11 in) lengths of embroidery thread. Sew the threads to the front, under the felt triangles. Plait the threads and tie together.

CHILD'S PATCHWORK SWEATER
· · · · · ·

This sweater is made of strips of different coloured squares knitted with simple motifs.
The strips are then sewn together into blocks. The finished seams are laced in white and the
border edged with pompons.

YOU WILL NEED
· · · · · ·

*1 x 25 g (1 oz) ball yarn
in six shades*

4 mm (No 8) knitting needles

pencil and squared paper

needle and matching thread

small amount of white yarn

crewel needle

70 cm (28 in) pompon tape

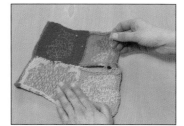

1
For each sleeve, knit two strips of two blocks. Pin and sew the strips together from the wrong side.

2
Lace the work on the right side over the joined seams using white yarn. Then lace across from left to right to separate the coloured blocks.

3
Neaten the edges by knitting two rows round the neck edge and lower sleeve edges. Sew the pompon tape round the bottom edge.

TO FIT: 61 cm (24 in) chest
ACTUAL SIZE: 68.5 cm (27 in)
LENGTH: 33 cm (13 in)
SLEEVE LENGTH: 23 cm (9 in)

PREPARATION

Tension: Worked in pattern on 4 mm (No 8) needles, 24 sts x 26 rows measures 10 cm (4 in). To obtain the correct tension, change the needle size.

Draw the motifs from the back of the book on to squared paper. Each block is 26 stitches by 28 rows. For the back and front, knit three strips of three blocks. Shape the front neck half way up the last centre block.

APPLIQUÉ SUNFLOWER

Appliqué a shiny satin flower on to the bib of a child's dress or dungarees (overalls). This simple motif is stitched by hand.

YOU WILL NEED
• • • • • •

paper and pencil

card (cardboard)

craft knife

scraps of iron-on interfacing

sharp scissors

iron

assorted satin scraps

dressmaker's pins

needle and matching thread

1
Iron the interfacing shapes to the back of the satin scraps. Cut out, adding a 5 mm (¼ in) seam allowance.

2
Turn under a hem on the raw edges, pin and tack (baste).

3
Position the motif on the garment. Pin and slip-stitch each section in place.

PREPARATION

Copy the templates on to card (cardboard) and cut out. Transfer each petal and the flower centre on to the interfacing. Cut out the shapes with a sharp pair of scissors.

FLOWER CENTRE
AND PETAL

KANTHA QUILT

This traditional method of echo quilting is used in India. Complex quilting patterns are formed by echoing the shapes of patchwork or appliqué motifs with a halo of tiny stitches, worked in two or more parallel lines.

YOU WILL NEED

paper and pencil

card (cardboard)

craft knife

dressmaker's scissors

*70 cm x 90 cm
(28 in x 36 in) wadding
(batting)*

*70 cm x 90 cm
(28 in x 36 in) muslin*

*1 m x 90 cm (1 yd x 36 in)
backing fabric*

*needle and tacking
(basting) thread*

vanishing marker

assorted embroidery threads

crewel needle

*sewing machine and
matching thread*

PREPARATION

Enlarge the templates and cut out of card (cardboard). Sandwich the wadding (batting) between the muslin and backing fabric and tack (baste). Mark a border 11 cm (4½ in) from the edges with a row of tacking stitches.

TO FINISH

Trim the muslin and the wadding (batting) by 2 cm (¾ in), then bring the backing fabric over to the top and bind the raw edges (see Basic Techniques).

1
Trace the paisley and bird motifs on to the quilt border. Find the centre of the quilt and draw a flower freehand, then trace the elephants in the centre square.

2
Work a neat back stitch round the outline of all the motifs using red embroidery thread.

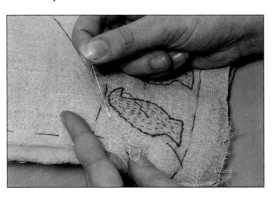

3
Work tiny running stitches inside each motif in various colours to echo the outline.

4
Using thread that matches the quilt, work tiny running stitches in a halo round each motif to echo the shapes filling the whole quilt.

PEACOCK AND
PAISLEY 50%

ELEPHANT
50%

Hawaiian Appliqué Hanging

Patchwork and appliqué were taken to Hawaii by missionaries in the 19th century, but it was the Hawaiians themselves who developed this unique method of appliqué. The motifs are folded and cut in the same way as paper snowflakes.

You Will Need
......

1 m x 90 cm (1 yd x 36 in) green cotton fabric

43 cm (17 in) square cream cotton fabric

dressmaker's scissors

spray starch

iron

30 cm (12 in) squared paper

pencil

paper scissors

vanishing marker

needle and matching thread

embroidery scissors

46 cm (18 in) square wadding (batting)

dressmaker's pins

embroidery hoop

quilting thread

crewel needle

Preparation

Cut the green cotton into two 43 cm (17 in) squares and a 10 cm (4 in) strip. Spray starch both sides of one green square and press. Cut three 10 cm (4 in) wide strips of fabric, fold the loops in half and stitch. Turn right side out. Enlarge the design from the back of the book.

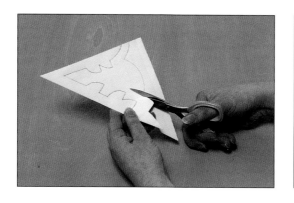

1
Fold the paper into quarters and then fold again into a triangle. Trace the design on to the triangle. Draw the border round the edge following the shape of the snowflake. Cut along the lines and open out.

2
Trace round the template on to the green square using the vanishing marker and tack (baste) to the cream square, 5 mm (¼ in) from the outline of the motif and 5 mm (¼ in) from the outline of the border.

3
Cut the green fabric a little at a time to 3 mm (⅛ in) from the pencil line. Snip the curves.

4
Press on the wrong side. Neaten the edges, turning under a small hem. Slip-stitch in place.

5
Sandwich the wadding (batting) between the appliquéd square and the green cotton, securing the loops. Pin and tack.

To Finish

Stretch the appliqué on an embroidery hoop. Starting at the edge, hand quilt halos round the snowflake. Work parallel rows of tiny running stitches round the border. Trim the edges of the square. Cut two strips of green fabric 10 cm x 38 cm (4 in x 15 in), and two strips 10 cm x 46 cm (4 in x 18 in). Stitch to the edges as borders (see Basic Techniques).

POTPOURRI CUSHION

Appliqué a scrap of fabric, Hawaiian style, on to an organza cushion and fill with sweet-smelling potpourri. Decorate with old linen buttons and use as an air freshener or relaxing pillow.

YOU WILL NEED

paper and pencil

20 cm (8 in) square organza fabric in two colours

dressmaker's scissors

needle and tacking (basting) thread

vanishing marker

embroidery hoop

sewing machine and matching thread

sharp scissors

potpourri

linen buttons

1

Centre the organza in the embroidery hoop. Set the machine to darning mode, and work a straight stitch all round the marked outline.

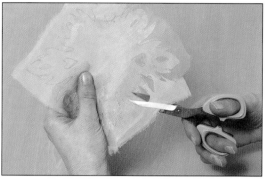

2

Trim away the excess top fabric. Work several more lines of stitching over the first, to cover the raw edge fully.

PREPARATION

Cut a piece of paper 16 cm (6¼ in) square. Fold in half, and in half again. Fold one corner to its opposite, and draw on the motif. Cut out. Tack (baste) the two squares of organza together. Position the paper template and transfer the motif.

TO FINISH

Tack (baste) together the two remaining organza squares, and place them right sides facing the appliquéd piece. Make up the cushion (see Basic Techniques). Fill with potpourri and slip-stitch to close. Decorate the edges with linen buttons.

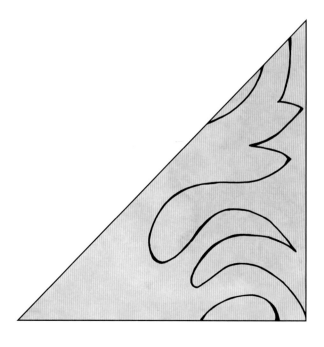

BEADED PURSE
· · · · · ·

This purse is appliquéd with fabric hearts which are embellished with beads and coloured threads. It fastens at the top with a loop and button.

YOU WILL NEED

12 cm x 32 cm (4 ¾ in x 13 in) blue fabric

dressmaker's scissors

12 cm x 32 cm (4 ¾ in x 13 in) red lining fabric

scraps of fabric for the hearts

scraps of iron-on interfacing

iron

embroidery hoop

needle and matching thread

assorted beads

sewing machine and matching thread

wooden button

red embroidery thread

PREPARATION

Fold the long ends of the blue fabric together and cut in half. Repeat with the red lining. Cut four large and four small contrasting hearts from the scraps and iron interfacing on to the back.

1

Using an embroidery hoop, appliqué two large hearts on to each blue square then appliqué two small hearts on top. Embellish with beads and decorative stitching. Right sides facing, machine stitch together.

2

Make a red lining and attach to the purse. Sew the button to the top of the purse. Plait six strands of embroidery thread, 20 cm (8 in) long, and tie with a knot. Stitch the plait to the back of the purse in a loop.

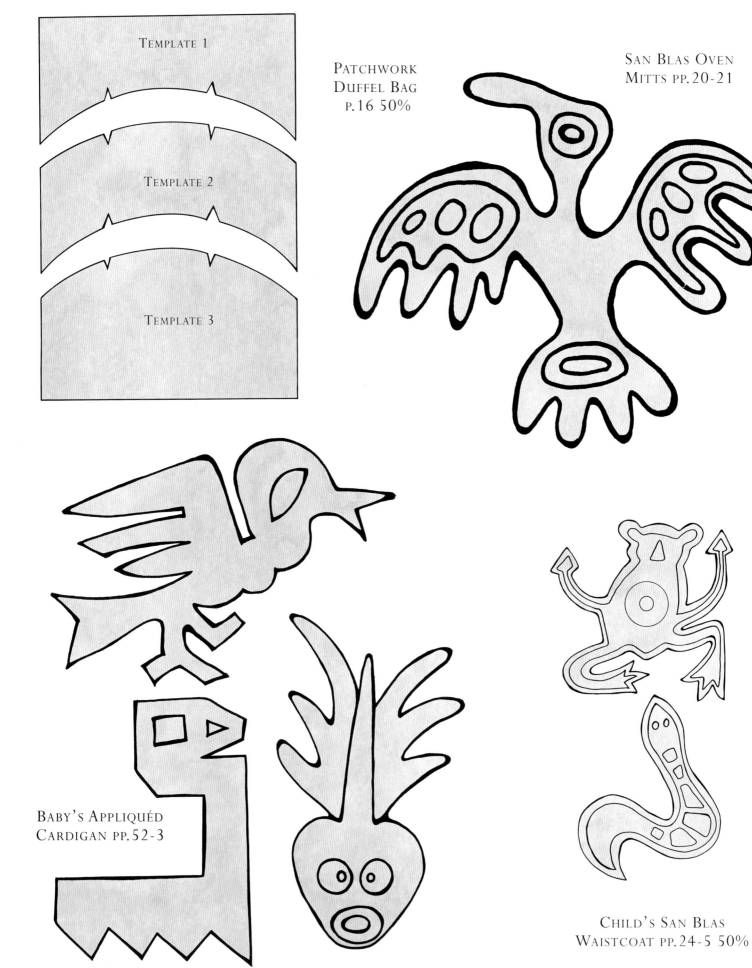

TEMPLATE 1

TEMPLATE 2

TEMPLATE 3

PATCHWORK
DUFFEL BAG
P. 16 50%

SAN BLAS OVEN
MITTS PP. 20-21

BABY'S APPLIQUÉD
CARDIGAN PP. 52-3

CHILD'S SAN BLAS
WAISTCOAT PP. 24-5 50%

PA NDAU
APPLIQUÉ FRAME
PP. 44-5

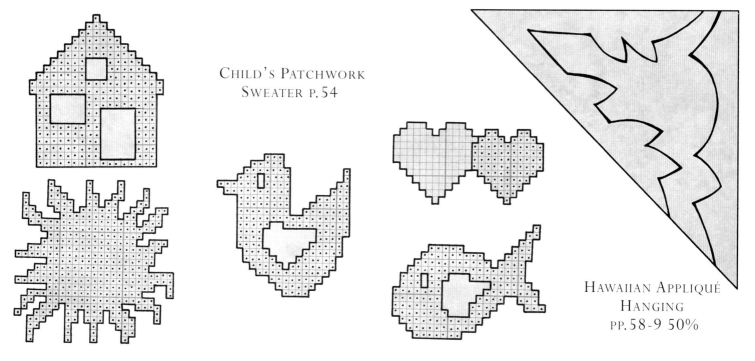

CHILD'S PATCHWORK
SWEATER P. 54

HAWAIIAN APPLIQUÉ
HANGING
PP. 58-9 50%

INDEX
· · · · · ·

ACKNOWLEDGEMENTS
· · · · · ·

The Publishers would like to thank the following craftspeople who designed and made the projects for this book: Louise Brownlow, Sally Burton, Rachel Frost, Sylvia Landers, Chloe Walker, Jenny Watson, Angela Wheeler and Dorothy Wood. With special thanks to Isabel Stanley for commissioning work and designing and making many of the projects. With thanks to Kay Dimbleby and her clients for permission to photograph the quilt on page 6 b. Additional photography by John Freeman, page 6 b, and Peter Williams, pages 6 t and 7.

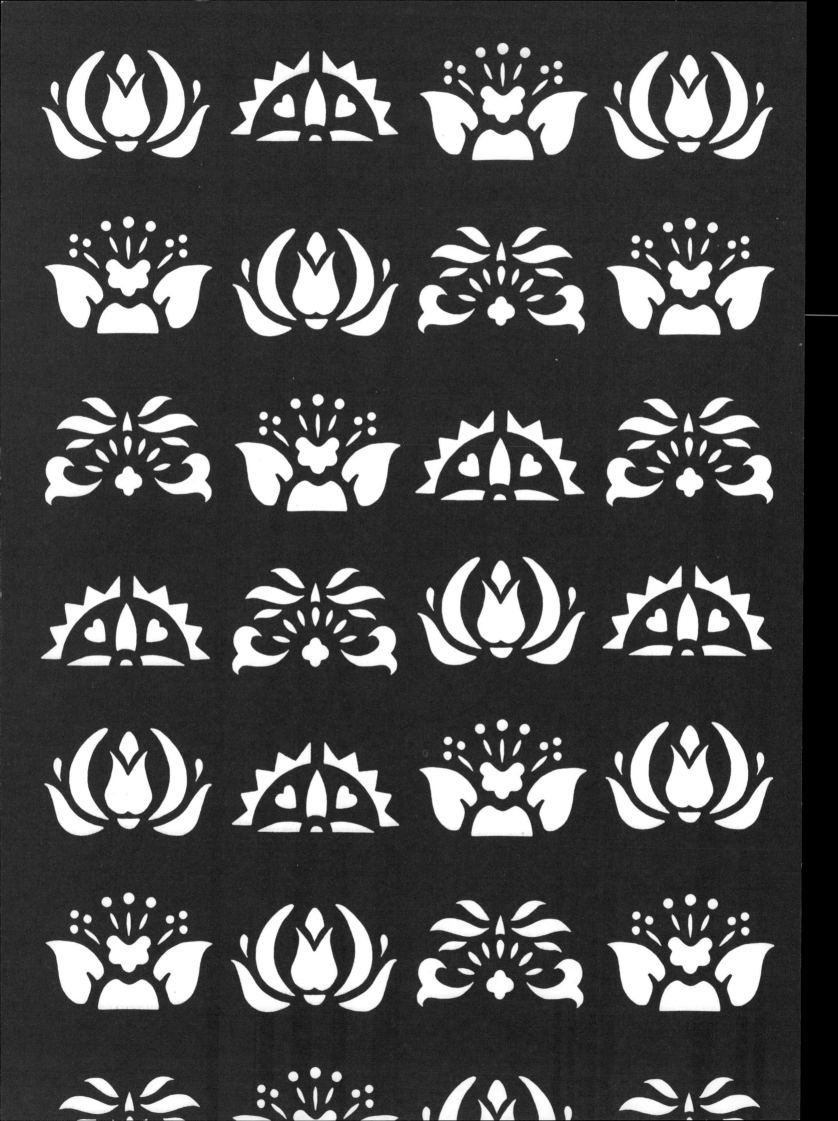